Let Me TELL YOU

A Collection of Poetry

GLENDA G. NIXON

authorHOUSE®

AuthorHouse™
1663 Liberty Drive
Bloomington, IN 47403
www.authorhouse.com
Phone: 1 (800) 839-8640

Published by AuthorHouse 05/18/2018

ISBN: 978-1-5462-4329-8 (sc)
ISBN: 978-1-5462-4328-1 (e)

Print information available on the last page.

This book is dedicated to my brother

Chauncey Leon Cherry

Acknowledgement

I would like to give honor to God for giving me the talent to write poetry. I also would like to thank my daughters Kenyatta and Cherisse for always believing in my writing. Thank you to my family for always calling on me whenever a poem was needed. To my best friend Elgin thank you for always giving me a topic to write about you were always an inspiration. I like to thank my brother in Christ Kenny for being so obedient. Last but not least I would like to thank Authorhouse publishing for giving me the opportunity to make my dream come true. There are numerous people I could write on this page but I am going to always be grateful for any and everyone that had a part in making this a reality.

Preface

I believe writing began for me when I started paying attention to the letters above the blackboard in elementary school. I remember vividly not paying any attention to my teacher as she struggled to teach my class.

I was to busy perfecting my handwriting so I could have the best handwriting in the classroom. Little did I know that handwriting would be my destiny. Once I figured out all the letters, I began writing poems.

My first poems started with "Roses are red, violets are blue", you remember those right? As I continued writing, my poems escalated from the roses saga to writing about how I was feeling. It was on then. I couldn't stop writing poems. I wrote about prejudice in high school and it was selected for the school newspaper. How about that?

As I got older I began writing about any and everything that was going on around me. I entered contest and won, I wrote a poem that was published in the book entitled Great Poems of Our Times. But still I wouldn't take the time to sit down and create a book of poems.

Then one day years later while at work, I saw a note on the bulletin asking for anyone who would be interested in writing for the new newspaper that was being published. I decided I was going to ask I if I could write a poem for the paper. I did, they loved it and asked if I could keep them coming.

My brother in Christ wasn't there that week so he had no way of knowing about my decision to write the poem or my book. One day as we was passing in the hallway he says to me,"you walking around here with all that intelligience and all that talent". I replied, "yeah I'm going to get that book out soon. He later told me that the Lord spoke to him on my behalf and had told him to tell me that I would write seventeen books.

Here is the first one I hope you enjoy your reading.

Woman

The finest art ever created. The most intellectual form stated.
The backbone of everyday living. The creature
who receives nothing but is always giving.
The body that carries a little child. The
mind that travels mile after mile.
The precious wonder of the world. No
longer a sweet and innocent girl.
Man was created first believe it yes you can. Then
God wanted better and there was woman.

Deadly Enforcers

Four white officers with nothing better to do decided
to pick on one of our brothers it wasn't me or you.
They said he had violated they just right out lied. They
beat and kicked him and pushed him side from side.
But someone captured the whole ugly scene. They saw
on video the beating of an innocent human being.
In and out of the courtroom jurors at a lost. Gave
the verdict acquitted LA paid the cost.
Back in the courtroom with the judge on the bench. If it had
been black officers the decision would have been lynch.
Chief of police says he wants peace in L.A. if theses
officers aren't convicted peace will seem very far away.
Wrong is wrong color doesn't matter. Make the right
decision before more blood has to splatter.

Cocaine

Smoking tooting shooting the caine. Your brain
is frying and your heart is in pain.
Gotta get that blast can't pay the rent. Forgetting
where all that bill money went.
After you finish you feel stupid as hell. Don't
have no one to talk to no one to tell.
Thinking about selling that pretty diamond ring. But
don't want nobody to think you're just a dope fiend.
Better leave that caine alone, cause the high gets old.
Remember you don't have anything everythings been sold.

Material Things

I don't need a diamond or a brand new car to
let me know that Jesus isn't very far.
I don't need a pretty dress or a pair of shiny shoes
to assure me his love I'm never going to lose.
I don't need a bank account or a trip to Rome
to be with Jesus and have a happy home.
I don't need a fancy restaurant or the finest wine
to be content and have a peace of mind.
What I need is to praise him with respect and
then dear Jesus my life will be set.

Underserved Respect

Sometimes I feel you don't deserve the respect you get.
Sometimes I feel like you don't deserve the time I've spent.
One would assume your priorities are in tacked. They
would be oh so surprised if they knew the known fact.
Selfishness slide into a giving soul. No warm
blood runs in the heart-only cold.
You could make a gentle person turn into a snake. The
gentleness the caring could easily turn from genuine to fake.
No denying the truth will ever set you free. This
ugly side of you is positively scaring me.

Jesus is Right by Your Side

He feels your pain he knows your sorrow. He's here for
you today so you don't have to worry about tomorrow.
Your tears are his, your heartbreak is shared. Just in
case if any doubt you wondered if he cared.
He worries when you worry he feels just as low as you.
His heart is working diligently knowing what to do.
You don't ever have to feel alone its not a lonely ride. To share
your sorrow tears and pain Jesus is right by your side.

Experienced Feeling

I don't like this feeling I feel sorta down. I can't seem
to make a smile only a sad looking frown.
Nothing bad has happen I guess its just one of those days.
I hope it decides to leave I hope it's not one that stays.
In a way it's kinda of scary I don't seem to know just why.
The laughter is so far away I just feel like I want to cry.
Everyday can't be sunny, life just isn't that way. I pray that
it gets better because this is such a lonely sad day.
But I won't let it get me down for tomorrow I
may be able to smile. I'll accept this feeling as an
experience and close my eyes to rest a while.

How

How do you say goodbye to a heartfelt love? How
do you change the color of a snow white dove.
How do you let of when the hold is so tight? How
do you stop loving when it doesn't feel right?
How can you prevent the tears from staining your face?
How can you call all the time spent a senseless waste?
How can you erase the happiness you shared?
How can you say you never really cared?
How will you face life without that everyday glow?
How can you stop saying yes and finally say no?

I'm Going to Make It to The Top

I've been set back but not for long. I thought I
would never make it but I was wrong.
I had all kinds of trouble from people I thought I could
trust. Don't trust anyone Glenda and that's a must.
But things are looking better and I just can't wait.
Because now I know that it's never too late.
I'm going full speed ahead and I'm not going to stop.
Because I know I'm going to make it to the top.

Yesterday

The time flew by the moments grew shorter.
I was happy for the time being.
I truly believed you loved me. I truly believed you were my friend.
I trusted you with my life. I honored your honesty to the utmost.
The time flew by the moments grew shorter.
I was happy for the time being.
I believed, I trusted I honored I was happy…Yesterday.

Black Changes

Black, beautiful full of pride. They said we
wouldn't overcome man how they lied.
Things were bad some of us failed. The beatings
the abuse all the cotton we bailed.
They called us slaves we got no respect. There's
still some out there who hasn't realized yet.
Our bodies were tired our hearts were low. There
was a world of freedom and we must go.
They called him master yes sir please. We'll work
in your kitchen for outside we'll freeze.
Times have changed things have progressed.
Sorry ex-master for we must rest.

Glenda

I know Glenda very well right now her life is confused
as hell. She can't make up her mind on what she
wants but sooner or later she'll make her point.
She has really never changed from being that shy little girl
or being afraid of all the things in this great big world.
I know she doesn't want to hurt anyone or make them
sad. She has fantasized life and that makes her glad.
Her life has been many of ups and down hills. And
she knows she'll make it better if it's her she has to kill.
She wants to live right and be treated the same. If they
all turn against her it would be a crying shame.
She has had many she has called her friends. And
none of those friendships has she wanted to end.
I'm not saying that she doesn't make mistakes. I'm saying
her life will get better whether she gives or takes.

The Gulf War

I never would have dreamed of living through a war. Thank
God I lived through this one I pray there is no more.
Families are not sleeping going through mental anguish both day
and night. Asking God to please let their loved ones be alright.
Kuwait Iraq titles that won't leave our minds. Thinking
of the troops praying peace they will find. Yellow
ribbons draping showing support wherever we go. We're
proud of our warriors and we want them to know.
They're coming back our hearts are glad.
The ones we lost our hearts are sad.

Aids

Hours of pleasure sweet passionate love made. Not
once thinking your partner could have AIDS.
Sharing the needle passing the syndrome on. Forgetting about
the little baby that have to be born. AIDS will kill protection
is a must. Don't be fooled by that one night of lust.
One partner is all you need the risk is very high. Being
with more than one partner could be your ticket to die.
Being stared at by the ones who just don't understand.
Trying hard to discredit you as fast as they can.
It have to be discussed we can't make it go away.
We have to fight this deadly disease or
with our lives we'll have to pay.

Wasn't Looking for Love

The strangest thing happen I was completely surprised.
And there you were looking into my eyes.
The stare was intimate the smile was glowing. We
were made for each other without even knowing.
I think God must have known that I'd been lonely for too
long. And sending you to me couldn't of been wrong.
Like not knowing when the stars will shine above.
We happen when we wasn't looking for love.

My Life is Empty Without Jesus

The clouds are dark the trees are bare. Life
without Jesus make me not want to care.
The emptiness I feel is beyond any kind of pain. I
can't imagine anymore sunshine only rain.
I want to smile but the tears seem to fall. Without
you in my life Jesus I'm nothing at all.
I truly do love you my heart is in a spin. Please tell
me good Lord all my life where have you been.
I can't find anywhere to go Father nothing to do.
My life is just totally empty without you.

What's The Matter

Can you tell me what's the matter? Why are you
acting so shy? What is the problem why are you
acting if though you're going to die?
What have they did to you? What have they said? What
did they do to you to make you wish you were dead?
Why are you crying tell me what did they do?
Why are they trying so hard to destroy you?
Who are they what do they want? You have
explained to them and got to your point.
Maybe they'll leave maybe they'll go. But
until then we really don't know.

My Teenage Daughter

It seems so familiar that growing up thing. Letting
go of your parents and trying your wings.
Nothing ever seems to go just the right way. The debt
for life is due and you're the one who has to pay.
Acne, weight gain hair never looks right. Your mother
seems to be your enemy you two always have to fight.
Nobody understands how you really feel inside. It's your
childhood that's leaving not your precious pride.
But you must hang in there adolescence won't last for long. You
have to remember not to be weak you must always be strong.

Violence in The Black Community

Killing brothers stabbing your friends when
is this black violence going to end?
Can't play basketball unless someone has to die. The
news reporter says it was related to you being high.
You grew up together your house was his home. You sold
drugs for the white man now your buddy is gone.
Black on black crime brother is not the way. Let's
stick together and together let's stay.
Sto killing yur brothers and sisters we need them to go on.
We don't need the violence and we don't need to mourn.

I Have Dreams

I have dreams of what I want to do. And
I'm sure you have some too.
I find myself fantasizing of how it will be.
Everything falling into place for me.
My dreams are lovely happy and gay. But I'll
never get anything dreaming all day.
So I'm awake from my dreams and on my way
to make them come true for me today.

Life is Life

The emptiness inside is overwhelming. The emotions
are running wild. I'm lost in my own mind.
There's a fulfillment I must acquire. I must
achieve a happier disposition.
There's an unique craving for peace of mind.
Subconsciously the tears are overflowing.
However; life dishes out sour notes to be
sang. But nevertheless…Life is Life.

Hidden Love

I love you, you love me. We're deliriously happy.
The warm touch we feel when we're close.
You kiss me and I melt. I kiss you and you smile. Your
hands explore my body my hands explore yours.
You say,"I love you bae." I say I love you darling." When we're
not alone you glance at me and I know you want me.
We're deeply in love—and yet the love is hidden.

When I'm Alone

As I sit alone all by myself just thinking I have the
tendency to want to cry. I feel so left out of things
my mind just wanders and I want to die.
I have thousands of things on my mind from early ages
to the end of my time. I sometimes wish I could go back
and start all over again. That's what thinking does when
you think of now and wish you were back then.
Reading doesn't help because it'll usually pertain
to how you're feeling and you have to remember
it's loneliness with whom you're dealing.

Daddy

They said I looked exactly like you. The making
of me left little for my mother to do.
We didn't live together but we stayed in touch. You were
always a call away and I appreciated that so much.
I know you were proud of me you always told me so. There
was nothing you wouldn't do for me you never told me no.
Your love proved to me parents can live apart. I had
the biggest part of you your big loving heart.
The day you died made me very sad. But I knew
from the beginning I had the very best dad.

Friendship

We are friends and nothing is better than that. Our
friendship is like a jewel genuine. The first time I
saw you I had visions of us laughing together.
I am going to treasure this relationship forever
because its one of a kind. There's not confusion
and no false pretenses and I like all of that.
Never hestitate to tell anyone you have a good
friend because all of me is good.

Infidelity

First you fall in love then you get married. Away to the
honeymoon and through the threshold you're carried.
Only having eyes for you partner of life. Sharing
your entire world with your husband or wife.
Your vows were said within the heart you promised
to be faithful until death do you part.
But you strayed away now the love had been shared.
The spouse at home believed you cared.
Things get bad lies are told. Trust and respect infidelity stoled.

Kenyatta

Kenyatta Shaunte' born the first day of May. Seven pounds two
ounces twenty inches long. I thank God nothing was wrong.
Brown eyes, black hair, pretty as can be. I'm so
very proud because she's a part of me.
I'm her mother and I think she's great. Even though she
was suppose to be born in April she came a little late.
Now she's getting older and amazing me everyday. What a
wonderful and intelligent human being she is I really must say.
The birth of Kenyatta was a joy indeed. And with the
help of the Lord she'll have everything she needs.

Wondering

I'm wondering how things will be when I get older what
will I see? Things will be different things will change.
Things will look different from a whole new range.
You wonder if you will ever see how things will
change for you and me. You don't believe the things
they say but you'll see on that special day.
Things are getting worse can't you tell? We're
not living on earth we're living in hell.

If It Wasn't for My Lord

If it wasn't for my Lord I don't know where I'd be. If
it wasn't for my Lord I wouldn't even be me.
If it wasn't for my Lord I wouldn't have any guidance at
all. If it wasn't for my Lord I would just get up and fall.
If it wasn't for my Lord my whole life would be a mess.
If it wasn't for my Lord I would never get any rest.

Gift from Above

It's a rare given gift that won't get old. It's not
quite likely to receive on that will get stole.
All gifts should be treasured adored in its unique way.
They all have a special meaning that lasts day after day.
It really doesn't matter if the gift is large or small.
Gifts come in all sizes even short and tall.
But I've got an everlasting gift that was give with lots of
love. I've got that wonderful special gift from up above.

Unappreciative Love

I bend over backwards just to see you smile.
Your needs come first mine wait a while.
I put my heart into everything I do for you. My
world revolved around you I thought you knew.
How can someone who receives so much love
be so unkind? It's obvious you're not listening
to you heart or what's left of your mind.
I don't ask for much I try to get along. I guess
my way of loving you is totally wrong.
Maybe you've chosen an incompatible mate. Things will never
be the same again because you're trying to turn love to hate.
You think I'm wrong when I lay beside you and cry.
You think it's a joke when I say I want to die.
But put yourself in my place when all you do is give. You
wonder why you're being mistreated you wonder why you live.
I'm not a phony person I can only be me. I thought
our love was strong enough to classify us as we.
When my prayers are said I ask the mighty one above
to give me a strong not an unappreciative love.

Scared of Happiness

I would think after all the years of sadness I
would welcome a life of gladness.
But I never can be susre of the danger I'm in. I'm
so scared of losing I'm too afraid to win.
I feel the happiness trying to possess my heart.
I neglect the feeling before it starts.
I want to trust but my minds say no. My
aching heart say give it a go.
I'm afraid to love cause it hurts so bad. Being
scared of happiness is really sad.

Other Emotions

Not so wonderful being angry with you. Emotions
are a wreck and I don't know what to do.
Thinking ugly things about the man I love. Asking
for forgiveness from the mighty one above.
I want to say I'm sorry but the pride get in the way.
Wanna look into your eyes and beg you to stay.
Emotions are funny things telling you what to do.
Emotions are serious things we have to work through.

Cherisse

I know this little girl her name is Cherisse. She's
such a wonderful daughter sister and niece.
She doesn't look her age her mind is very advanced. She
has a lot of talents and likes to sing and dance.
She has the prettiest brown eyes the most sunniest smile.
She's her own little lady with a most unique style.
She enjoys her life she won't settle for less. She's
very persistent and she strives to be the best.
You'll have to meet Cherisse she's one of a kind. And
I'm so very lucky because Cherisse is mine.

August 2015

I believed in my heart we was meant to be. I was
feeling you and you were feeling me.
I felt it was real I still really do. I have no
idea why I can't stop loving you.
We kicked it for a while but I pushed you away.
Now with my broken heart I'll have to pay.
I made a fool of myself trying to get you back.
I guess my persistence was a little slack.
When the time is right the outcome will be revealed. My
heart will be saddened or my heart will be healed.

I'm Ready

I'm ready and have been for long. I'm ready to do
right and not wrong. I I'm ready to reach my special
goal. I m ready to be good successful and bold.
I've been ready for such a longtime, I've really thought
about it and made up my mind. I'm ready to go, I'm ready
to start. I'm ready to do it from the bottom of my heart.
I've reached my goal and I'm happy too. I didn't only
do it for me I did it for you. I've made up my mind I'm
here at last. I'm looking to the future not the past.

My Mother

Everyone has a mother either living or at rest. But no
matter where their mothers are my mother is the best.
From birth to this day now your mother has been around. From
birth to this day now my mother has never let me down.
Mothers are special and mothers are sweet. But when
it comes to my mother she just can't be beat.
Today is Mother's Day for mothers near and far. But
out of all the other mothers my mother is the star.
I say these words with help from the Lord above.
Happy Mother's Day, Mother with all my love.

Where Did It All Go

Things started out good but they seemed to drift away. I
thought we has a relationship that would last day after day.
But you lied to me and made me cry. You
hurt my feelings and that's not lie.
I'm very serious as I can be by me crying I guess you can see.
I wanted to make you happy I wanted to make you smile.
I wanted to make everything for us just a little while.
Tell me what did I do for you to tell me it's
over for you to tell me we're through?
I told you I loved you did you understand
you tell everybody you're a man.
You might say she won't find out but that's not so.
I know a lot of things baby you don't know.
You try to run a game you think you're cool.
Baby please remember I'm no fool.
Yeah she cries but that's alright. When you look
for her she's gonna be out of your sight.
She's gonna get ahead she's going straight. When
you as for her back it's gonna be too late.
So sorry my friend I hate to say you hurt
her now and she's gone away.

No Need for Jealousy

I don't want another lover it wouldn't be the same. Being
with another would be like playing a silly game.
The kiss would be different the hug would be a bore. The
thought of another would knock me to the floor.
The intimacy would be a joke the respect would be a
lie. If you're aren't my lover I'd just rather die.
There's no need for jealousy you're the man for me.
There's no need for jealousy I love you so let it be.

Special Friends

I think it's so wonderful the way we smile. Sometimes
we forget we're lovers for just a little while.
We can talk about anything but we have our private thoughts.
Neither one of us are perfect like all we have our faults.
We don't understand why couples want to fight. We
laugh and talk and try to make everything alright.
Everyone think it's amazing the way we get along. We look
inside for the good things and work on the wrong.
If you understand life from its beginning to end. Then
you'll understand what we mean by being special friends.

No More Let Downs

I feel let down by the man that mean so much to me.
My mind is confused locked up and I don't feel free.
I think he has stop loving me I think he's thrown the trust
away. I think he want to leave but I'll beg him to stay.
I let him down sometime too. But I never stop
loving him or having trust in what he do.
Maybe if we stop and thought of each other ways. We wouldn't
let each other down and have a lot more better days.

Strongly Together

I'm so content my life is grand. The love is
back between me and my man.
Confidence is restored trust is strong.
Our love will last for very long.
I'm so thankful I'm truly blessed. My
heart and mind can finally rest.
I have no fears the doubts have faded. I thank God that I waited.
I will not let any cause keep us apart. The love
will remain strong from the very start.

When You're Not Here

Have you ever been alone on a rainy day? And you
felt like nothing was ever going to go your way.
Have you ever been in a big house all alone? And you
felt like the walls the air and everything was gone.
Have you ever felt like you have no friends at all? And
if you did they would pick you up and let you fall.
Have you ever been in a crowd and felt like no one was
there? And even if they were you didn't think they cared.
And when you're not here I feel all of these ways.
And those are the times I wish for better days.

No Lies

You were one in a million I couldn't believe my eyes. You
were honest from the beginning there were never any lies.
I became your friend the moment we met. You respected
me like no other and you haven't changed yet.
You have your priorities in order you made me understand. You
cared about me but for me not to forget you're still a man.
I fell in love you said you couldn't. I know you had
good reason or said that to me you wouldn't.
But it's been a while and we're still friends. I
pray that is something that never end.

Special

Our hearts were locked but yet was taken. A
beautiful relationship had been awaken.
It's very special because we didn't try at all. We were
hiding our feelings behind a concrete wall.
The union is open the honesty is great. We
have a friendship that will not wait.
Faithfulness has no question love is no dim light.
Together we makeit through wrong or through right.

The Years

For eight years of my life I have been involved with you. It
was hard exciting and a very special relationship too.
We have gotten this far and my love has grown. And I think
God must have known to keep us together through smiles
and tears. And to love one another for all these years.
The years we have spent together mean so much to me. I
find being honest and dedicated the only way to be.
I'll never lie or hurt you again and I'll be there
until the end. I'll always love you forever in a day
because loving you there's no better way.

Am I Enough

As time goes on life isn't easy for us. We go through
tough ordeals but deal with them we must.
Sometimes I feel nothing I do is ever right. Keeping
this relationship together is a mighty hard fight.
I'm aware that some things I do is really off key. I don't
deliberately do bad things I just have to be me.
I question your motives for treating me cold. It's like you're
looking for a new love because mine is getting old.
The world isn't an easy place to be things can get very rough.
But my love for you is real my question is am I enough.

Can I Come First

I always have to wait why must I come last? I'm
living here in the future not in the past.
Sometimes I need attention I need to come first. I'm
tired of feeling bad I feel like I'm the worst.
Does everyone have to be important does everyone have to
be the one? Why must I always be left out of all the fun?
I'm suppose to be the first I'm suppose to be your girl.
Sometimes you make me feel I don't exist in this world.
Stop treating me this way it makes me feel bad. I'm
the one you love at least that's what you said.
For your love I feel such a thirst I need to know I come first.

What Do I Have to Do

What do I have to do to make you understand that
I really care? What do I have to do to make you
understand there's only one way to be fair?
What do I have to say to make you understand that
you are my heart? What do I have to say to make
you understand without you it won't start?
How do I have to act to make you understand I'm
woman enough? How do I have to act to make
you understand I'm tender and not tough?
How od I make you understand any of these things?
Write talk or maybe sing. I'm sure you do I know you do
I know you can because you're no child you're a man.

We Talked

It made me sad to hear your voice. The
love I had somehow got lost.
It was confusing the you sound it was quite
sure your happiness had been found.
I got the message it wasn't a mistake. And the
best of it you were going to make.
I'm glad you're happy, I want you to be. But
not with anyone else just with me.

A Reserved Heart

I have always loved you you have always been number one.
You carved a reserved place for yourself in my heart.
That place has been broken a many times before. And yet
it mends itself back together in time for some more.
If it would be said that I don't have a forgiving heart then
you become my attorney and defend me during that part.
It's like you own my heart with a repeat version of "Break
Don't Break." I am of human flesh and I too get tired.
Please don't waste your life using my heart to fall
back on. You'll soon crush it and it'll be gone.

I'll Wait

The news hit me like a two by four. My heart
stopped and it fell to the floor.
I knew it was coming I thought I was prepared.
That's when I realized how much I really cared.
I wasn't really angry maybe just a little mad. I
wanted to be your Mrs oh so really bad.
I do love you and you mean the world to me.
And that's the way it'll always be.
So my love I'll wait right here and never forget I love you dear.

When We're Together Again

I can't wait for that beautiful day that we
share our happiness in every way.
There will be no more lies and no more tears.
Life will be great without anymore fears.
We won't worry about what people say. For
we'll be together day after day.
We'll live in harmony and share all the fun. No one
can ever stop us because we would have won.
All the scars that we have created we'll mend. For
that special day when we're together again.

Life Goes On

I didn't want to live when you said goodbye. I knew
most of the reasons I didn't have to ask why.
I begged you to stay but your mind was set. I
gambled on a good thing and I lost the bet.
I'll never forget you you were so special to me. To
bad I didn't listen to bad I couldn't see.
The thought of not seeing you everyday is sad. But
thinking of the times I saw you I'm more than glad.
Together a beautiful relationship was born.
But it's over now and life goes on.

Printed in the United States
By Bookmasters